TAKING YOUR BAND ONLINE

SIMONE PAYMENT

rosen publishing's
rosen central

NEW YORK

Published in 2012 by The Rosen Publishing Group, Inc.
29 East 21st Street, New York, NY 10010

Copyright © 2012 by The Rosen Publishing Group, Inc.

First Edition

Library of Congress Cataloging-in-Publication Data

Payment, Simone.
Taking your band online/Simone Payment. — 1st ed.
    p. cm. — (Garage bands)
Includes bibliographical references and index.
ISBN 978-1-4488-5660-2 (library binding) —
ISBN 978-1-4488-5664-0 (pbk.) —
ISBN 978-1-4488-5668-8 (6-pack)
1. Music — Internet marketing — Juvenile literature.
2. Music — Vocational guidance — Juvenile literature. I. Title.
ML3790.P39 2012
780.285'4678 — dc22

                                                    2011015238

Manufactured in the United States of America

CPSIA Compliance Information: Batch #W12YA: For further information, contact Rosen Publishing, New York, New York, at 1-800-237-9932.

CONTENTS

INTRODUCTION 4

CHAPTER ONE
BEFORE GOING ONLINE....7

CHAPTER TWO
WEB SITE BASICS....16

CHAPTER THREE
UPLOADING YOUR
CONTENT........31

CHAPTER FOUR
ONLINE PROMOTION...44

- GLOSSARY............................ 53
- FOR MORE INFORMATION..... 55
- FOR FURTHER READING....... 58
- BIBLIOGRAPHY 60
- INDEX................................... 62

INTRODUCTION

Music is a basic and universal form of human expression. People around the world enjoy listening to—and making—music. It is not too common to meet people who say they don't enjoy music. But some people are passionate about music. Anyone reading this book probably falls into that category.

Teenagers have been forming bands for years. But the Internet has changed almost everything about being a musician and being in a band for teens and adults alike. The Internet has made it easier for musicians to connect with each other. They can find other musicians

AS THEY SAY, "THE INTERNET IS NEVER CLOSED," SO FANS CAN DISCOVER NEW MUSIC ANY TIME OF DAY, ANY DAY OF THE WEEK.

who love the same band or type of music. They can discover new music by a band in another country. Guitarists can find drummers or singers in their hometown who are looking to form a band. Bassists can find other bassists to teach them a new technique—online or in person.

Perhaps the most important change the Internet has brought about is that it allows bands to connect directly to fans. Before the Internet, it was difficult for teen bands to find an audience outside of their friends, family, and class-mates. Now, nearly anyone can record music and then post it for the world to hear. Bands can communicate directly with fans and get feedback from them. They can instantly find new listeners or make current fans even more passion-ate about the music.

The Internet has put bands in charge. Bands used to have to rely on record labels to put out their music and market it to the public. Although bands can still sign with a record label and become successful, it is just as easy to become successful and then sign with a record label. Or not. It's up to a band to decide. While this freedom allows bands to possibly write their own ticket to stardom, there are some drawbacks. It can take a lot of time and effort to make a band a success. Also, there are a lot of bands out there, all of them competing for listeners' ears. However, with hard work and some creativity, it is within reach to build a successful band.

BEFORE GOING ONLINE

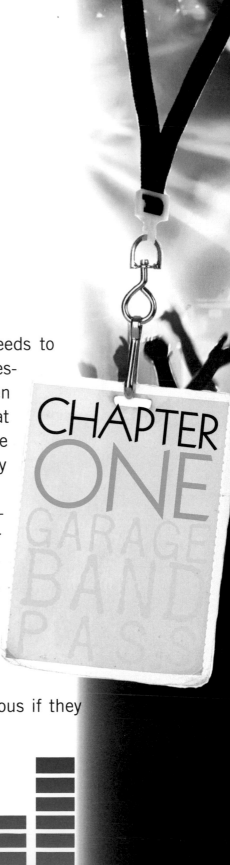

There are many things a band needs to consider before building an online presence: Who will be in the band? How often and where will the band practice? What will the band be named? How will the band record music? Will the band play live? If so, where and how often?

Some people want to be solo musicians. They have a clear vision for their music and aren't interested in collaborating with others. Other musicians believe it is a lot more fun to play with other people. Being in a band can be beneficial because there are other people to help make decisions. Some people also feel less self-conscious if they make music as part of a group.

START-UP BANDS ARE OFTEN CALLED "GARAGE BANDS" BECAUSE MANY ACTUALLY PRACTICE IN A GARAGE. BUT THE TERM CAN REFER TO ANY BAND THAT IS NOT YET PROFESSIONAL.

To find other band members, talk to friends—and friends of friends. Ask a music teacher at school or someone who gives lessons at a local music school. Post a notice on online bulletin boards or bulletin boards at music schools, practice spaces, or other places where musicians hang out. Be specific about what kinds of instruments the band will include and what kind of music the band might play.

Setting Ground Rules

For a band to be a success, members have to get along. One of the best ways to ensure that this happens is to be sure that everyone is on the same page. The way to do this is to set clear ground rules. Don't assume that bands can make up rules as they go along—this can easily lead to fights.

BANDS CAN USE SEARCH ENGINES, SUCH AS GOOGLE (HTTP://WWW. GOOGLE.COM), TO HELP FIND A USED BASS GUITAR, PRACTICE SPACE, A T-SHIRT MANUFACTURER, OR OTHER BANDS' WEB SITES.

Decide as a group how often, and when, the band will practice. Of course, things like illness, school projects, and soccer games will interfere with the practice schedule at times. Still, commit to the practice schedule. For a band to succeed, all members need to be dedicated.

Discuss how serious the band members want to be about the band. Is everyone playing just to have fun? Or does the band intend to become internationally known? Everyone should have the same basic idea of the band's goals.

WITH A LITTLE HELP FROM FRIENDS

Band members can't necessarily do everything themselves when first establishing themselves and building an online presence. It's great if the bassist is also a videographer who can record shows, but sometimes no one in the band knows how to use a video camera. Or maybe the band needs help getting the drum kit to a show or designing the band logo. That's when it is time to get help from friends or family members. Get the word out about what the band needs, say, on a social networking site. Ask friends at school, have family members ask their friends, or talk to teachers at school.

When the band finds someone to help, be clear about what is needed. For example, will this task take an hour or two days? Does the band need one photo or twenty? Think of ways to repay the volunteer for the help. Maybe the band can "pay" with homemade cookies or with free band T-shirts. Always make sure to thank volunteers, and credit their work on the Web site.

Disagreements are bound to happen, so think about how to settle them. Will the band take a vote? Have a discussion? Remember that it's important to be patient and flexible. Also, be supportive of other band members.

Practicing is an important step in becoming a great band, so finding a good practice space is essential. Try to find a space that everyone in the band can get to easily. A garage or basement can be great but must be soundproofed. Remember that if the band is practicing in someone's home or garage, it is important to be respectful of family members and neighbors. If they ask the band to stop or turn down the volume, do so right away or risk losing the practice space.

There are buildings that rent practice space to bands. Some storage facilities rent space as well. In some cases, there are age limits at these spaces, and most usually charge money. However, it is sometimes possible to share rental practice space with another band or bands. It might also be possible to practice in the music room or other area at school.

Naming the Band

A band name can represent the band's music, or it can be totally random. However, it is best to choose a name that is catchy so that people will remember it. Also, since you will be online, try to pick a name that people can easily search

MANY GARAGE BANDS, SUCH AS THIS ONE FROM CLEVELAND, OHIO, GET THEIR START BY PERFORMING AT THEIR SCHOOL'S BATTLE OF THE BANDS COMPETITION.

for. To choose a band name, you can get ideas from dictionaries, song lyrics, television shows, maps, or movies.

Keep a few things in mind when choosing a name. The name should be easy to spell so that fans will easily be able to find the band when using search engines like Google. Don't choose a band name that's already in use because the other band can sue if they can prove that they had the name first. Also, don't use the full name of a person, especially someone

RAISING MONEY

Being in a band and building an online presence can be expensive. There are instruments to buy, practice spaces to rent, T-shirts to make, and many other expenses such as Web hosting and design. One way to make money is to sell band merchandise like stickers, posters, and T-shirts. Most of these items can be made inexpensively. With a little creativity, it is possible to make them at home. Another way to make money is by playing shows, but not all shows are paid gigs. If the band is playing a free show, put out a container and ask people to contribute. Or play on the street or another public place and put out a container for donations. Make sure to check local regulations about playing in public before you do this.

who is famous. It may be permissible, though, to use the full name of someone who is dead. To research band names already in use, check Google and music sites like iTunes.

Recording Music

Recording music at home—instead of in a professional recording studio—can be very easy. With just a computer and a recording device, it is possible to get decent-quality recorded music. Software, such as GarageBand, makes it easy to record and then mix music. It is also relatively easy and inexpensive to use a digital audio recording device. To record at home, the band will need a place to play and equipment, so think about where and how that can be done.

Another option is to use a professional recording studio. Because time in a recording studio is expensive, this is not always an option. However, some schools and colleges have recording studios. Recording time in these studios may be cheap or even free. For example, colleges that offer classes in music engineering or recording may offer free studio time so that their students can practice.

Playing in Public

Once a band has practiced a lot and knows how to play at least five to ten songs, it may be time to play in public. Finding a place to play can be difficult, but there are usually several options. Check local community centers, which sometimes offer opportunities for bands to play. Organize a show at school, or take part in a talent show. Check with local concert venues. Some offer afternoon all-ages shows. Some also put on "Battle of the Bands" events for teenage bands.

There are several logistical details to work out, such as how to get the band's gear to the show. Also, will there be sound equipment at the show, or must the band provide it? If the band will need its own equipment, it can be rented if the band doesn't own any.

When playing a show, make sure to follow a few guidelines so that the band will be invited to play more shows in the future. Be on time, and be prepared to play. Make sure to clean up when the show is over. And most important of all, play a good show. Don't waste the audience's time fiddling with equipment or deciding which song to play next. Play well and stay focused to make sure that there are plenty of shows in the band's future.

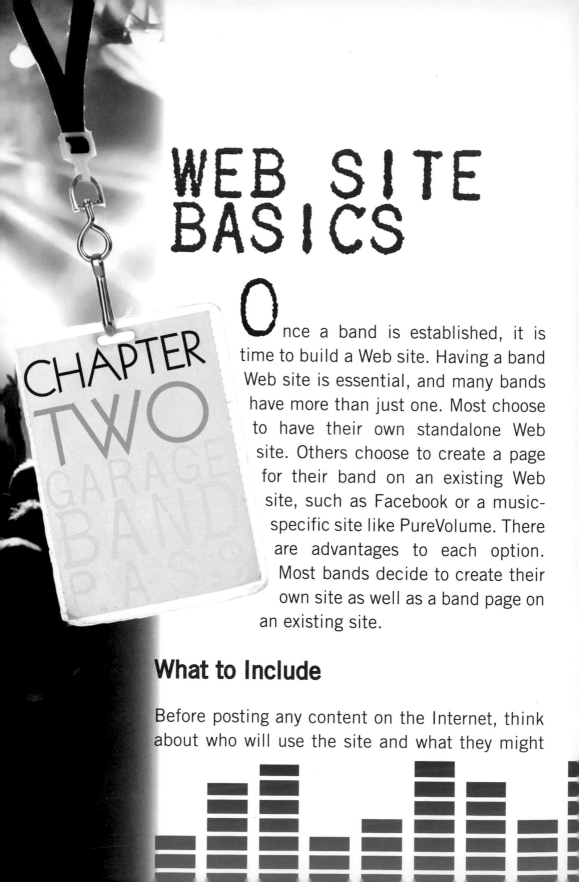

WEB SITE BASICS

CHAPTER TWO

GARAGE BAND PASS

Once a band is established, it is time to build a Web site. Having a band Web site is essential, and many bands have more than just one. Most choose to have their own standalone Web site. Others choose to create a page for their band on an existing Web site, such as Facebook or a music-specific site like PureVolume. There are advantages to each option. Most bands decide to create their own site as well as a band page on an existing site.

What to Include

Before posting any content on the Internet, think about who will use the site and what they might want to find there. Most bands post at least audio files, a band biography or history of the band, some pictures, and contact information. Band photographs, show dates, videos, news, and a store page are other options.

Do some research online, looking at as many band pages as possible. Make lists of the good parts—and the bad parts—of popular sites. Have discussions about these features and which ones will be important to put on the band's Web site.

Spend time thinking about the best ways for the band to showcase itself. Does the band wear costumes while performing? If so, make sure to include lots of photos on the Web site. Did the band come together in an unusual way? If so, make sure to include a band biography. Did a friend make a great music video of the band's most popular song? If so, post it on the site in a prominent location.

Once the band has decided what to include, start pulling the ingredients together. Make a list of all the elements that will be included—audio files, videos, text, and so on. (The next chapter includes more information about all of the elements of the site.) Discuss what will be on the home page and how many other pages there will be. Think about where each feature of the site will go. Decide how pages will be connected to other pages. For example, will there be a separate page for videos? If so, will that page connect to other pages within the site? Or will that page simply allow the site user to return to the main page after watching the videos?

DO PLENTY OF WEB RESEARCH BEFORE BUILDING THE BAND'S WEB SITE. A WELL-PLANNED SITE IS MUCH EASIER TO BUILD AND MAINTAIN.

With a list of what will be included and a plan for where everything will go, it is time to decide where on the Internet this information should be posted. Will the band have its own Web site or a page on an existing Web site?

Using an Established Web Site

An advantage to creating a band profile on an existing music site or social networking site is that it is free. That can be a major advantage to a band just starting out. Another advantage is that it is easy for existing fans to find you and new fans to discover you. Using an existing site also has the advantage of not being too complicated. The band won't need to buy a domain name. Nobody in the band will need design skills or need to learn any computer software.

However, there can be drawbacks to posting a band profile on a music or social networking site. One disadvantage is that not every site is around—or popular—forever. MySpace was once an extremely popular Web site that many bands used as a way to post music and reach out to fans. Although many bands still have MySpace pages, MySpace is no longer the popular social networking site it once was. Not as many music fans use it to discover new music or keep up with their favorite bands. Also, companies go out of business, not necessarily due to lack of popularity. If a band only has a page on one music site and that site goes out of business, the band's presence on the Web is gone.

facebook

Facebook helps you connect and share with the people in your life.

USING ESTABLISHED SOCIAL NETWORKS SUCH AS FACEBOOK (HTTP://WWW. FACEBOOK.COM) IS A GREAT WAY TO PROMOTE YOUR BAND TO AN EXISTING AUDIENCE.

Another disadvantage of using an existing site as the band's only Web site is that it might not allow the band to be too creative. Existing sites have specific features. A band that wants to add a special feature might not be able to do so.

For bands that decide to use an existing music or social networking site, there are many to try. Social networking sites like Facebook can be a good place to start. Band members may already have a good network of friends on the site, so once the band gets its page set up, it's easy to quickly and easily spread the word and build a fan base. Bands may also choose to post to one or more music-specific sites. Do research to decide which site or sites would be best for the band. Ask friends and other musicians what music Web sites they use and like. Find out where popular bands have profiles. Search out sites that specialize in a type of music that matches the type the band makes.

With a list of Web sites to post the band's profile on, start putting up band information. Each Web site has different procedures for posting, but most are easy to use. It is also free to register and post on these sites.

Carefully consider how many sites on which to post band information. While it is a great idea to post to several different sites to increase band exposure, it also requires a lot of work. If band pages are on several sites, each time a change needs to be made, it will need to be made multiple times. New songs, show dates, and other new information will have to be posted to every site on which the band has a profile.

Creating Your Own Web Site

Creating a new Web site for the band from scratch takes a little more work, but most bands decide this is essential for the band's success. It can also be a fun process. The first step is to get a domain name. A domain name is, in simple terms, the address at which Internet users can find a site. There are several sites that help users check whether or not

WEB SAFETY

Although the Internet is a terrific tool for a band, it does have some draw-backs. It is essential to do a few things to safeguard the safety of band members. Don't post any band members' home addresses. If the band decides to post a physical address, set up a post office box for the band. Don't use any band members' personal e-mail addresses. It is easy to set up a band e-mail address at free e-mail sites like Yahoo! and Google. Finally, don't agree to meet anyone in person who contacts the band and offers to help promote the band, record music, and so on. Do research to see if the person is legitimate. Ask a parent or teacher for help with this. If this offer is legitimate, only agree to meet with the person with a parent or other adult present.

a domain name is available. If the name is available, users pay a small fee to register the name. This allows users to buy the domain name for a specified amount of time, usually one year. Remember that to keep a domain name active, the fee must be paid every year. Shop around for Web sites that register domain names. None are free, but most are inexpensive. The price can vary depending on what the domain name ends with— for example, .com, .net, or .org. A few registration services to try are GoDaddy.com, Domain.com, and BlueRazor.com.

Think carefully about what domain name to register for the band. Of course, it's best to try to use the name of the band. If the name is already taken, try adding a word at the end, such as "band" or "music." Adding "the" at the beginning of the name may be another option to try. But keep in mind that it should be as easy as possible for fans to find the band's site. Therefore, it is not a good idea to use hyphens, misspellings, or a name completely unrelated to the band.

Once the band has a domain name, find a Web host. This is a company that provides the virtual space for the band's Web site to "live" on the Internet. A hosting company stores all of the files that make up the Web site. It will usually provide

DOMAIN REGISTRAR SITES, SUCH AS GODADDY (HTTP://WWW.GODADDY.COM), MAKE IT EASY TO PURCHASE A UNIQUE URL FOR YOUR BAND'S WEB SITE.

e-mail addresses linked to the Web site. These sites are not free. They may charge by the month or per year.

Try to find a Web hosting company that gives plenty of bandwidth because the band will probably want to post music and videos, which require a lot of bandwidth. Some sites specialize in hosting bands, so they have features that are helpful for musicians. These features might include audio players or tools to create and manage e-mail newsletters. They also offer plenty of bandwidth. Music hosting sites include HostBaby.com and ReverbNation.com.

Develop the Site

With a domain name and a place for the band's site to live, the next step is to design the site. There are two types of design software: site creation and content management systems. Both types have advantages and disadvantages. The band can decide which type to use based on skills that band members might have, or whether anyone in the band knows other people who can help with the band's site.

The first type of software for Web designing is site creation software. An example is Adobe's Dreamweaver. Site creation software has lots of features. It allows users to create complex, interesting designs. It is great if someone in the band knows how to use it or can spend a lot of time learning the program. Or if someone in the band has a friend or family member who knows it—and is willing to help design the site—it can be great to design a site this way.

However, in addition to requiring time and specialized knowledge, site creation software has another drawback. When using this software, the design of the site and the content contained in the site are linked. And all of the design and content files are stored on the computer of the person who uses the program. So when it is time to make an update or a change to the site, only the person who has access to that computer can do so.

Content management systems, on the other hand, separate design from content. This type of system stores files on the Internet. This allows anyone to make changes or updates to the band's Web site (as long as they have a password). An example of a content management system is WordPress. In general, content management systems are easier to learn and use than site creation software. The drawback is that it is not as easy to create unique designs with a content management system.

In addition to the two types of Web site creation software, there are companies that have templates that bands can use to create their Web site. Bandzoogle.com and Squarespace.com are examples of sites that offer a variety of templates. The drawback to this method is that there is usually a monthly charge.

Have a band discussion about which method to use and who might be able to build the Web site. If it is a band member, make sure that the other members of the band take on some responsibilities so that all of the work is not left to one person. For example, if one band

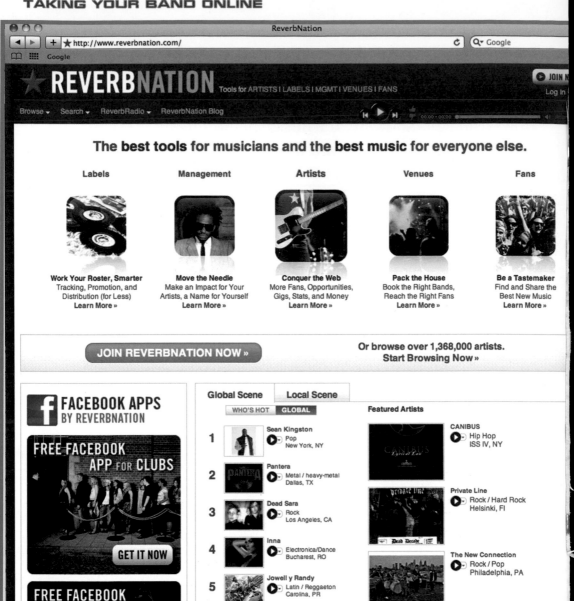

SOME MUSIC HOSTING SITES ALSO OFFER OTHER SERVICES HELPFUL TO BANDS. FOR EXAMPLE, REVERBNATION (HTTP://WWW.REVERBNATION.COM) HAS A FREE FEATURE THAT HELPS BANDS FIND PLACES TO PLAY LIVE.

Of course, the most important thing to post on the Web site is the music. Get audio files on the site as soon as possible. This may seem obvious, but people want to hear what the band sounds like. A band can have a perfectly written description of their music on the Web site, but unless someone can hear it for himself or herself, that person is not likely to know whether he or she likes the band or not. So one of the first priorities should be posting audio files.

Try to include videos. They don't need to be fancy or of the highest quality. Have someone in the band set up a video camera during rehearsal and post some of it online. Have a friend or family member record the band at a local show and post a song or two. Or make a video of the newest song. Videos are just another way to let fans know what the band is all about.

Keep in mind that although it is great to have lots of interesting features, it is important not to overdo it. It should be easy for fans to find what they are looking for and get from place to place on the site. Keep things simple. Simple doesn't have to mean boring. It is possible to design a site that is both creative and informative. Remember, too, that a Web site should be easy to read. There are lots of fun fonts that can be used, but just choose one or two. Make sure that the font is readable and large enough. People shouldn't have to work hard to read the site. If they do, they're not likely to stick around or

member is going to build the Web site, anoth(
be in charge of writing the band bio and anoth
take photos.

If the band decides to find someone else to b
Web site, be clear about what is expected o
designer. Be specific about what should be in
the site and who will provide the elements, suc
files or photos. If a friend or family member
out, keep in mind that the person is doing t
favor in his or her spare time. Have realistic e>
about when things will get done.

Keep track of all the content that will be on
who has what. Make a list or spreadsheet so th
knows who is responsible for each element.
item is stored or located should also be on th
Web site grows, keep the list up to date.

Tips for Success

There are a lot of bands out there and a lot (
Web sites. To have a successful site, it shou
different from all the other sites that are (
creative and express band members' pers(
the personality of the band, on the Web
features, great photos, and fun videos w
talking about the band and they'll keep c(
the Web site.

visit the site again. Also keep in mind that people are access-ing the Web from smaller and smaller screens, such as on smartphones or tablet computers. That is just another reason to keep the design simple.

Another important tip is to frequently add new material. This will keep people coming back to the site. No changes

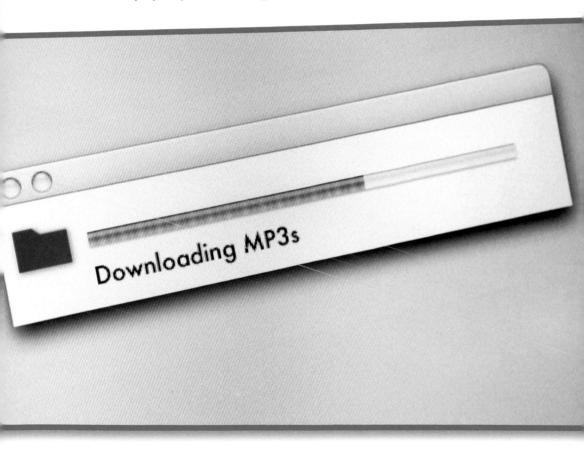

SOME BANDS CHOOSE TO ALLOW PEOPLE TO DOWNLOAD SONGS FOR FREE FROM THEIR WEB SITE. SOME ONLY ALLOW FANS TO LISTEN ONLINE, WHILE OTHERS CHOOSE TO DO A MIX OF THE TWO.

to the site can cause fans to lose interest or wonder if the band is still together. Post new songs, videos, pictures, and any other content as often as possible. Make sure that show dates are current. Let people know about new songs that the band is writing. Post exciting news or additional information about band members. Ask fans to write in with their questions and then post answers to these questions. Have fans send in their photos of the band from concerts or even rehearsals. Keep things fresh, and fans will keep visiting the site.

UPLOADING YOUR CONTENT

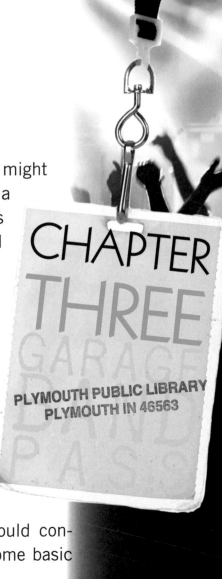

CHAPTER THREE

A flashy Web site with a great design might attract a fan's attention. But to keep a fan's attention, a nice-looking Web site is not enough. A good site must be backed up with great content.

In addition to music and pictures of the band, good written content about the band is an important component of the Web site. Clear and well-written information about the band is a way to let people know that a band is serious. Use the biography to tell the story of the band. The biography doesn't have to be dry and boring. In fact, it is a great idea to make the biography colorful and interesting. However, the biography should contain clear and complete information. Some basic

SOME SITES, SUCH AS ITUNES (HTTP://WWW.ITUNES.COM), TAKE PART OF WHAT ARTISTS MAKE SELLING THEIR SONGS. IT'S IMPORTANT TO CAREFULLY CHECK TERMS AND CONDITIONS BEFORE UPLOADING SONGS TO SELL.

questions that the biography should answer are: Who are the band members, and what instruments do they play? How did the band come together? How long has the band been playing together? Has the band played any shows? What kind of music does the band play? What are the band's goals?

Band members can write the biography or ask friends or family for help. Ask a teacher at school or a writer for the school paper to take a look at the draft and make suggestions. Carefully proofread the biography to correct any spelling and grammar mistakes before posting it to the Web site.

Contact information for the band should also be complete and correct. A band e-mail address is probably the most important piece of contact information. Remember not to use a band member's personal e-mail account for the band. Create a band e-mail address, and remember to check the e-mail account regularly. Including a snail mail address on the contact information page is optional. It is a good idea to include one if people will be sending things to the band through the mail. However, don't use a band member's home address. Ask a parent to set up a post office box for this purpose.

Music Files

Most of the time, music files are what new fans and old ones are coming to the band's Web site to find. It isn't necessary to have all the band's songs online, but at least two or three should be posted at all times. The band may decide to continue to post new songs as they are recorded, adding to what is already there. Or old songs can be taken off the site as new ones are added.

Think about how music will be provided on the band's Web site: Will downloading be allowed? Or should the music just stream on the site through a music player? Streaming allows users to listen but not download. Most Web hosting packages, especially specialized music ones, include a way to stream music on the site. Also decide where to post songs. Will songs be posted only on the band's Web site or on other sites as well? If the band has information at multiple locations, will the same songs be posted at each location? Or will songs be spread around, with different songs on each site?

When preparing music files for the Web, consider how to compress them. The MP3 is the most common music file type and can be used by most Web sites. If the band plans to post music files on multiple Web sites, MP3s are recommended. Another advantage of using MP3s is that the band name and song title can be embedded in the file. If available, a picture or band logo can also be added to the file. This is helpful if the files will be downloaded to fans' computers, phones, or other devices because the information about the file will be included.

Tags can be added in music software programs like iTunes and Windows Media Player. Make sure that both the band name and the song title are spelled correctly and attached to the correct file. Add as much information to the file name as possible, and try to be consistent in the way that files are named. For example, if the band's name is long, use a shortened form of the name, and use that same shortened name on all files.

PLENTY OF MUSIC FANS HAVE DISCOVERED A NEW FAVORITE BAND BY SEEING A VIDEO ON YOUTUBE (HTTP://WWW.YOUTUBE.COM). SO CONSIDER SHOOTING AND POSTING A VIDEO AND ADDING NEW ONES PERIODICALLY.

Videos

It is not essential to have videos on the site, but they can be a great way to help fans get to know the band better. In addition to posting videos on the Web site, it can be a good idea to post videos on video-specific sites like YouTube. Sometimes bands only post videos to an outside video site because videos can take up a lot of bandwidth. In this case, simply post a link on the band's site to the video.

Videos can show off the creativity of a band. There are many options for what type of video to make. Footage of the band practicing or playing a show is one type. A video could show a day in the life of the band. This could consist of short clips of band members at school, at practice, getting their equipment to a show, and so on. A music video could show off the band's acting skills, telling a story to go along with one of the band's songs. Or a music video could showcase other creative skills. For example, if a band member or friend of the band is an animator, he or she could animate a song or two. A video might also tell the story of how the band met and started playing together. Band members and other people involved with the band could be interviewed, and then the story can be pieced together.

Some technical skill and equipment are needed to make a video. However, fancy equipment and software aren't essential. It is possible to rent a video camera if no one in the band owns one or can borrow one. Schools, after-school programs, or community centers often offer video classes. Band members could take classes to learn the basics. Or ask friends or family members who might have taken a class for help. Sometimes students need to make a video for a class project, and a band video could be that project. Post flyers at school or at local community centers or colleges asking for help making the video.

THE MCLOVINS: A VIDEO SUCCESS STORY

The teenage band the McLovins from Hartford, Connecticut, found success by posting a video online. The band's three members met at music camp, and although they all go to different high schools, they began playing together in their free time. While learning to play together, they practiced cover songs, including "You Enjoy Myself" by the band Phish. They posted a video of themselves playing that song. In a very short time, there were more than ten thousand views of the video. It almost immediately drew attention to the band, even from members of Phish. As a result of the video, the McLovins have played music festivals. They have even been featured on *Rolling Stone* magazine's Web site.

Photos and Art

Photos are a great way for people to get to know the band. Posting at least one clear, high-quality photo of the whole band is important. This photo could be used by a music blog, local newspaper, or music publication that wants to feature the band. In addition to the band photo, post as many other photos as possible. These could include informal shots of the band playing a show, rehearsing, or just goofing off. Pictures of the band's instruments, the practice space, or the van the band uses to get to shows can give fans a look behind the scenes.

BANDS TODAY NEED MORE THAN INSTRUMENTS. SOME BASIC EQUIPMENT SUCH AS A CAMERA AND COMPUTER ARE TOOLS THAT EVERY BAND SHOULD OWN OR BE ABLE TO BORROW.

The photos on the Web site don't have to be taken by a professional. Ask friends or family members to share their pictures. Be sure to ask permission to use these photos before posting them to the band's Web site. Also ask the photographer how he or she would like to be credited on the Web site. Include that information near the photo.

Photos taken on digital cameras can be downloaded directly to a computer. The photos can then be prepared for posting on the Web with photo editing software. Make changes, such as cropping the photo or fixing problems like red eye. Most photo editing software has settings for saving the updated photos for the Web. JPGs and GIFs are the usual formats used on Web sites.

Photos don't have to be the only type of artwork on the Web site. If band members or friends of the band are cartoonists, painters, or illustrators, use artwork to illustrate the site. Don't forget to include the band's logo if one has been created.

CREATING A LOOK

Although music should be a band's number-one priority, creating a great look for the band can be important. Coming up with artwork and a band logo can be fun, and it can be an essential part of the band's identity. Aim for artwork that is eye-catching and represents the band and its music well. Try to make sure that band artwork is similar on all band products, such as T-shirts, posters, and stickers. It is a good idea to use the same font and pick a few colors to represent the band. If no one in the band is creative, ask friends, classmates, or family members for help. Or hold a fan contest to come up with the band's logo or T-shirt design.

Blogs

Blogs can be a fun way to communicate with fans. It is easy to include a blog as part of the band's Web site. A blog can help keep content on the site fresh and interesting. Write about anything happening with the band: new members, reports from rehearsals, song ideas, plans for the band, upcoming or past shows, or reviews of other bands' shows. One drawback of a blog is that it can take time to keep it current. However, band members can take turns writing entries for the blog.

Lyrics

Having a page for song lyrics is not essential, but some fans like to be able to find out what the band's songs are about. The lyrics can be posted simply as text. Or get a little more creative and handwrite and illustrate the lyrics. Then take a photo of the handwritten lyrics and post them. Or use design software, such as Photoshop or Illustrator, to create digitally illustrated lyrics. Make sure to proofread the lyrics—or ask someone else to—before posting them.

Press

A band just starting out might not have any articles written about them yet. But as soon as someone else has written about the band, consider starting a press section on the Web site. Even if it is an article in a school newspaper, post it to the Web site. This can show that the band is serious about its music.

On the press page, list the title or subject of the article and when and where it appeared. Post the full text of an article or just a link to an article if it has appeared online. If only a link is included, write a brief description of the article as a teaser to get fans interested in clicking through to it. Remember to get permission from the writer or publication to post or link to the article.

Your Online Store

A great way for a band to raise money is to sell things online. However, there are a few things to consider before deciding to sell band merchandise on the Web site: How will people pay for merchandise? Who will ship items to buyers, and how will that be done? What kind of things will the band sell in the store? How will the band figure out how many of each item to sell? Consider all of these questions before building an online store for the band's Web site.

One of the most widely used ways to accept online payments is to go through PayPal. This is a way for people to pay with a credit card or through a bank account. Buyers will need to have a PayPal account to purchase items from the band's store. It is easy and free to set up a PayPal account. However, PayPal does collect a fee from sellers, and the fee depends on how much is sold per month.

Another way to sell merchandise is through an external Web site, such as eBay.

Make sure that there is an easy way for the band to ship items like T-shirts or posters. Be clear about who will pack and ship the items. Be sure to charge sellers an appropriate amount for postage, and think about how to package items so that they will not be damaged during shipment.

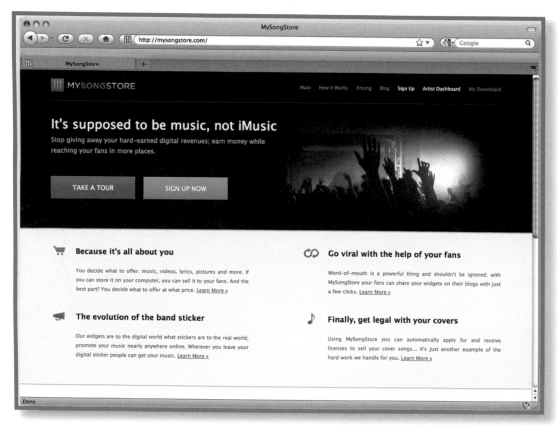

EXISTING WEB SITES SET UP TO SELL INDIVIDUAL SONGS CAN SAVE A BAND THE TIME AND EXPENSE OF SETTING UP THEIR OWN ONLINE STORE. MYSONGSTORE.COM (HTTP://WWW.MYSONGSTORE.COM) IS ONE SUCH SITE.

Think carefully about what to sell and how many of each item will be available. If the band decides to make T-shirts, how many should be made? In which sizes and which colors? Who will pay for them to be made? What will the band do if T-shirts sell out in one hour, or if no T-shirts sell at all? One way to avoid these concerns is to sell T-shirts on a print-on-demand Web site, such as CafePress. Print-on-demand sites keep the band's artwork on file and then print T-shirts only as fans order them.

It is possible to have a store that only sells music files. Bands will still need to have a way for fans to pay for the music, but they won't need to figure out how to ship items or how many products to make. Some Web sites, such as MySongStore.com and Soundation.com, allow bands to sell their songs online from the sites. These sites can be linked to the band's Web site.

Another option in a simple online store is to have a way for fans to make donations. An online payment system like PayPal will allow fans to make donations.

ONLINE PROMOTION

CHAPTER FOUR GARAGE BAND PASS

Finding a band's Web site can be easy...if someone already knows about the band and where to look. But getting people who don't already know the band to the Web site takes some work. With a little extra effort, it is possible to bring new fans to the Web site to check out the band.

Social Networking

One of the best ways to get people to visit the Web site is by using social networking. The more people who know about the band, the more interest in the band will build. As more people become interested in the band, they will tell their friends, who will tell their friends.

THROUGH FACEBOOK AND OTHER SOCIAL NETWORKING SITES, A BAND CAN END UP WITH FANS FROM ALL OVER THE WORLD.

There are many types of social networking that a band can use. For example, set up a Twitter account and tweet about new songs or videos. Post band photos to a Flickr page, with links to the band's Web site. Tag the photos with as many terms as possible so that more people will find them when doing searches. Use Facebook to get the word out about upcoming

45

shows. Ask fans to add the band's songs to their playlists on Facebook so that their friends can be introduced to the band's music. Post "Name Our New Song" contests on Twitter or Facebook with links to the Web site. Be creative about finding ways to let more people know about the band and getting them to visit the Web site.

Search Engines

If people are looking for the band online, it is important for them to be able to quickly and easily find the band's Web site. To make sure that people find the band when searching online, it is a good idea to submit the band's URL to search engines, such as Yahoo! and Google. Check each search engine's main page for instructions for submitting a URL. Only the URL of the band's main page needs to be submitted. It is free to submit a URL to a search engine.

Blog Coverage

Music blogs can be a great way to expose people to the band's music. Some music blogs have a few thousand readers, but others have hundreds of thousands of readers. Getting the band's music on a popular music blog can bring in plenty of new fans.

To get started, search the Web for music blogs that focus on a similar music style. This is because a country music blog is not likely to feature songs from a metal band,

GROWING AND MAINTAINING AN ONLINE PRESENCE FOR A BAND CAN TAKE A LOT OF TIME AND ENERGY. HOWEVER, IT CAN BE A PATH TO BAND SUCCESS, MAKING IT WELL WORTH THE EFFORT.

for example. Once the list has been narrowed down to a few blogs, check the contact information on each one and follow submission rules carefully. Most blogs ask for submissions via e-mail. Submit songs along with a polite and professional

47

SOCIAL NETWORKING SAFETY TIPS

When making a band profile on a social networking site, be careful about linking it to band members' personal profiles. It can be easy for people whom the band doesn't know to get personal information from those profiles. If band members do want to link personal profiles to the band profile, set privacy settings so that only friends can view personal profiles. Or consider making personal profiles that don't include any identifying information, such as last names, school names, or addresses.

letter. The letter should provide basic information about the band, including a brief bio and a description of the music. Focus on what makes the band and the music special. This will help the blogger write about the band as well as the music. It is a good idea to follow up a few weeks after submission if there has been no response. Be persistent, but be careful not to be a pest.

Podcasts

Another way to get the word out about the band is to do podcasts. Bands can do their own podcasts or be guests on someone else's podcast. Podcasts can be put out on a regular schedule, such as once a week or month, or only occasionally. While creating a podcast is relatively easy, it does take time. This is especially true of podcasts that aim to come out regularly.

Podcasts can be posted on a page of the band's Web site, as well as on any band pages on other sites. They can also be made available through podcast sites like iTunes.

Lyrics Sites

Song lyrics Web sites can be another way to draw attention to the band. It is easy to submit lyrics for inclusion on a site, such as Lyrics.com and A-ZLyrics.com. These sites have a "Submit" button and a simple upload process. Some require membership,

TWO OF THE BEST PARTS OF BEING IN A BAND CAN BE SHARING YOUR LOVE OF MUSIC WITH FRIENDS AND BAND MATES AND DISCOVERING NEW MUSIC.

but it is free to join. Some lyrics sites also feature music files, and some have a social networking component. Take advantage of all of these features as another way to promote the band.

Mailing Lists

Mailing lists can be a great way to stay in touch with fans. They can keep fans up to date on new songs, shows, and any other band news. Provide the important information in the mailing list message, such as show times and locations, but also include the URL for the band's Web site so that fans can get additional information.

CAREERS IN THE MUSIC INDUSTRY

There are plenty of ways to work in the music industry, whether or not you're a musician. Managers handle all kinds of details for bands. Recording engineers work with a band during the recording process in the studio. This job requires some technical know-how and a good ear. Producers also work with the band and the recording engineer in the studio. Their job is to get the best possible sound out of the recording process. Record label owners run a business that gives bands money to record or go on tour. In turn, they get part of whatever the band earns. Booking agents set up tours for bands. They usually work for more than one band. For example, a booking agent might work for a record label and set up tours for all the bands on the label. Just some of the other ways to work in the music business are as a music writer; a roadie; or a DJ for a radio station or a club, or for events like weddings.

Include a page on the band's Web site (or sites) where fans can sign up for the mailing list. Most Web hosting services provide a mailing list feature. Another way to add fans to the mailing list is to sign them up in person at shows.

Keep in mind that there are many ways to reach fans besides a mailing list. Use Twitter or blog posts, for example, to get the word out about new songs or events. Bands can use

TWITTER (HTTP://WWW.TWITTER.COM) CAN BE AN EASY WAY TO STAY IN TOUCH WITH FANS AND PROVIDE QUICK UPDATES, SUCH AS A LAST–MINUTE CHANGE OF VENUE.

many methods to ask fans to get involved and spread the word about the band's music. Remember to ask nicely if you are requesting that fans do something, such as add a new song to their playlist. Also, don't bombard fans with messages. This can overwhelm them and turn them off of the band.

Use any and all of the tools that the Web has to offer. Promote the band actively and creatively. Hard work can pay off, and nearly any band can become the next big thing.

GLOSSARY

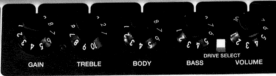

ANIMATOR   A person who creates an animated, or moving, cartoon.

BANDWIDTH The rate at which data can travel.

CROP To make a digital image smaller by cutting out extra details around the edges.

DIGITAL AUDIO RECORDING DEVICE A small portable device that can record sound.

DOMAIN NAME The primary Internet address for a Web site.

GIG   A concert or event for which a band is hired to perform.

HOME PAGE The first page that a user encounters on a Web site.

LOGISTICAL   Having to do with handling many details associated with an event.

MERCHANDISE Any material offered for sale.

PRINT-ON-DEMAND The act of printing only those items that someone has already ordered.

PROFILE Basic information about a person (or band) posted to a Web site.

RED EYE   The condition in which a person's eyes show up as red in a photograph; it's usually caused by using a flash.

REGULATION   A law or rule.

ROADIE   A person who works for a band, moving and setting up equipment.

SOFTWARE A computer program.

SOUNDPROOF   To insulate in order to keep sound in.

SPREADSHEET A computer program that can store and sort data.

SUE   To take legal action against someone.

TAG Identifying information such as band name and song title added to sound files.

TEASER   A short excerpt that can make a reader want to find out more.

TEMPLATE   A ready-made pattern into which a user puts his or her own content.

FOR MORE INFORMATION

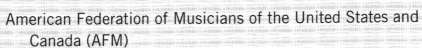

American Federation of Musicians of the United States and
    Canada (AFM)
1501 Broadway, Suite 600
New York, NY 10036
(212) 869-1330
Web site: http://www.afm.org
AFM represents professional musicians. It also has several
    programs and scholarships for young musicians.

American Society of Composers, Authors and Publishers (ASCAP)
One Lincoln Plaza
New York, NY 10023-7142
(212) 621-6219
Web site: http://www.ascap.com
ASCAP is an organization that represents musical artists,
    composers, songwriters, and music publishers.

Canadian Musical Reproduction Rights Agency (CMRRA)
56 Wellesley Street West, #320
Toronto, ON M5S 2S3
Canada
(416) 926-1966
Web site: http://www.cmrra.ca
CMRRA is an organization representing music copyright
    owners in Canada.

National Association for Music Education (MENC)
1806 Robert Fulton Drive
Reston, VA 20191
(800) 336-3768
Web site: http://www.menc.org
MENC is an arts education organization focused on music
    education.

Plugged In Teen Band Program
146 Warren Street
Needham, MA 02492
(781) 956-4281
Web site: http://www.pluggedinband.org
Plugged In teaches teens everything they need to know about play-
    ing in a band. It also shows how bands can give back to the
    community by raising money for various causes.

Rock 'n' Roll Camp for Girls
P.O. Box 11324
Portland, OR 97211
(503) 445-4991
Web site: http://www.girlsrockcamp.org
Rock 'n' Roll Camp for Girls runs summer programs for girls who
    want to form bands or who already have. It also offers coaching
    and mentoring for girl bands who want to improve their music
    and message.

SchoolJam USA
c/o NAMM
5790 Armada Drive
Carlsbad, CA 92008
(760) 438-8001

Web site: http://www.wannaplaymusic.com/schooljam-usa/about
The School Jam USA program is a free, yearly national competition
    open to bands with members between the ages of thirteen and
    nineteen.

Web Sites

Due to the changing nature of Internet links, Rosen Publishing
has developed an online list of Web sites related to the subject of this book. This site is updated regularly. Please use
this link to access the list:

http://www.rosenlinks.com/gaba/onli

FOR FURTHER READING

Anderson, Marisa (ed.). *Rock 'n' Roll Camp for Girls: How to Start a Band, Write Songs, Record an Album, and Rock Out*. San Francisco, CA: Chronicle Books, 2008.

Baker, Bob. *Guerilla Music Marketing Handbook: 201 Self-Promotion Ideas for Songwriters, Musicians and Bands on a Budget*. St. Louis, MO: Spotlight Publications, 2007.

Bove, Terry. *iLife '11 for Dummies*. Hoboken, NJ: Wiley, 2011.

Chertkow, Randy, and Jason Feehan. *The Indie Band Survival Guide: The Complete Manual for the Do-It-Yourself Musician*. New York, NY: St. Martin's Griffin, 2008.

Crossingham, John. *Learn to Speak Music: A Guide to Creating, Performing, and Promoting Your Songs*. Toronto, Canada: Owl Kids Books, 2009.

Frauenfelder, Mark. *Rule the Web: How to Do Anything and Everything on the Internet—Better, Faster, Easier*. New York, NY: St. Martin's Press, 2007.

Hoole, Gavin, and Cheryl Smith. *The Really, Really Easy Step-by-Step Guide to Building Your Own Website for Absolute Beginners of All Ages*. London, England: New Holland, 2009.

Hopper, Jessica. *The Girls' Guide to Rocking: How to Start a Band, Book Gigs, and Get Rolling to Rock Stardom*. New York, NY: Workman Publishing, 2009.

Hudson, Noel. *The Band Name Book*. Ontario, Canada: Boston Mills Press, 2008.

Hussey, Tris. *Create Your Own Blog: 6 Easy Projects to Start Blogging Like a Pro*. Indianapolis, IN: SAMS, 2010.

Johnson, Arne, and Karen Macklin. *Indie Girl: From Starting a Band to Launching a Fashion Company, Nine Ways to Turn Your Creative Talent into Reality*. San Francisco, CA: Zest, 2008.

Passman, Donald S. *All You Need to Know About the Music Business*. 7th ed. New York, NY: Free Press, 2009.

Poolos, J. *Designing, Building, and Maintaining Web Sites*. New York, NY: Rosen Publishing, 2010.

Selfridge, Benjamin, Peter Selfridge, and Jennifer Osburn. *The Teen's Guide to Creating Web Pages and Blogs*. Waco, TX: Prufrock Press, 2009.

Thomas, Andrew S. *Garage to Gigs: A Musician's Guide*. New York, NY: Billboard Books, 2008.

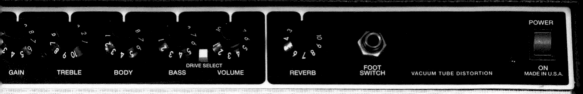

GAIN | TREBLE | BODY | DRIVE SELECT | BASS | VOLUME | REVERB | FOOT SWITCH | VACUUM TUBE DISTORTION | POWER | ON MADE IN U.S.A.

Anderson, Marisa (ed.). *Rock 'n' Roll Camp for Girls: How to Start a Band, Write Songs, Record an Album, and Rock Out.* San Francisco, CA: Chronicle Books, 2008.

Baker, Bob. *Guerilla Music Marketing Handbook: 201 Self-Promotion Ideas for Songwriters, Musicians and Bands on a Budget.* St. Louis, MO: Spotlight Publications, 2007.

Chertkow, Randy, and Jason Feehan. *The Indie Band Survival Guide: The Complete Manual for the Do-It-Yourself Musician.* New York, NY: St. Martin's Griffin, 2008.

Crossingham, John. *Learn to Speak Music: A Guide to Creating, Performing, and Promoting Your Songs.* Toronto, Canada: Owl Kids Books, 2009.

Hopper, Jessica. *The Girls' Guide to Rocking: How to Start a Band, Book Gigs, and Get Rolling to Rock Stardom.* New York, NY: Workman Publishing, 2009.

Johnson, Arne, and Karen Macklin. *Indie Girl: From Starting a Band to Launching a Fashion Company, Nine Ways to Turn Your Creative Talent into Reality.* San Francisco, CA: Zest, 2008.

Kot, Greg. *Ripped: How the Wired Generation Revolutionized Music.* New York, NY: Scribner, 2009.

Krolicki, Frank. "Ten Tips for Self-Promoting Your Indie Band." *Chicago Examiner,* March 4, 2009. Retrieved January 22, 2011 (http://www.examiner.com/rock-music-in-chicago/ten-tips-for-self-promoting-your-indie-band).

Mack, Steve, and Mitch Ratcliffe. *Podcasting Bible*. Hoboken, NJ: Wiley, 2007.

McLennan, Scott. "Homemade Jams: Are the McLovins the Next Great Force of Improv Rock?" *Boston Globe*, February 4, 2011, p. G24.

Nichols, Travis. *Punk Rock Etiquette: The Ultimate How-To Guide for DIY, Punk, Indie, and Underground Bands*. New York, NY: Roaring Brook Press, 2008.

Scott, David Meerman, and Brian Halligan. *Marketing Lessons from the Grateful Dead: What Every Business Can Learn from the Most Iconic Band in History*. Hoboken, NJ: Wiley, 2010.

Stim, Rich. *Music Law: How to Run Your Band's Business*. 6th ed. Berkeley, CA: Nolo, 2009.

Thomas, Andrew S. *Garage to Gigs: A Musician's Guide*. New York, NY: Billboard Books, 2008.

Vincent, Frances. *MySpace for Musicians: The Comprehensive Guide to Marketing Your Music Online*. Boston, MA: Thomson Course Technology, 2007.

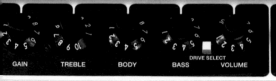

INDEX

A

Adobe Dreamweaver, 24

B

band members, finding, 7, 8
bandwidth, 24, 35
Bandzoogle.com, 25
"Battle of the Bands," 14
biography, 17, 27, 31–33, 48
blogs, 37, 40, 46–48, 50
BlueRazor.com, 22

C

content management systems, 24, 25

D

design templates, 25
digital audio recording device, 14
disagreements, 11
Domain.com, 22
domain name, 19, 21–23
donations, 13, 43

E

eBay, 42
e-mail, 22, 24, 33, 47

equipment

renting, 15
transporting, 10, 14, 36

F

Facebook, 16, 20, 45, 46
family, as band helpers, 10, 24,
    27, 33, 36, 39
Flickr, 45
font, 28, 39
friends, as band helpers, 10, 24,
    27, 33, 36, 39

G

GoDaddy.com, 22

H

HostBaby.com, 24

L

logos, 10, 39
lyrics, 12, 40, 49–50

M

mailing lists, 50–52
McLovins, the, 37

merchandise, 13, 41–43
money, raising for your band, 13
MP3 format, 34
music industry careers, 50
MySongStore.com, 43
MySpace, 19

N

naming your band, 7, 11–13

P

Paypal, 41, 43
performing, 7, 13, 14–15, 28, 36,
    37, 40, 46, 50
photo editing software, 39
podcasts, 48–49
practice, 7, 10, 11, 28, 36, 37, 40
press, 37, 40–41
print-on-demand sites, 43
PureVolume, 16

R

recording, 6, 7, 13–14, 22
recording software, 14
recording studio, 13, 14
record labels, 6, 50
ReverbNation.com, 24
rules, establishing for your band, 9–11

S

search engines, 46
site creation software, 24–25

social networking, 10, 19, 20–21,
    44–46, 48, 50
Soundation.com, 43
Squarespace.com, 25

T

Twitter, 45, 46, 50

V

videographer, 10

W

Web host, 23–24, 34, 51
Web site
    creating your own, 16, 21–24
    developing a, 24–27
    music, 17, 28, 24, 30, 31,
        33–34
    online store, 17, 41–43
    photos and art, 17, 27, 30, 31,
        37–39, 40
    safety, 22
    tips for success, 27–30
    using an existing site or network,
        16, 19–21
    videos, 17, 24, 27, 30, 35–36, 37
    what to put on it, 16–19, 40–41
WordPress, 25

Y

YouTube, 35

About the Author

Simone Payment has a degree in psychology from Cornell University and a master's degree in elementary education from Wheelock College. She is the author of twenty-six books for young adults. Her book *Inside Special Operations: Navy SEALs*, also from Rosen Publishing, won a 2004 Quick Picks for Reluctant Young Readers award from the American Library Association and is on the Nonfiction Honor List of Voice of Youth Advocates.

Photo Credits

Cover Jupiterimages/Brand X Pictures/Thinkstock; cover and interior background image (club), pp. 18, 47 Shutterstock.com; p. 5 Tetra Images/Getty Images; p. 8 DreamPictures/Taxi/Getty Images; p. 9 © www.istockphoto.com/Chris Hutchinson; p. 12 Gus Chan/The Plain Dealer/Landov; pp. 20, 51 Nicholas Kamm/AFP/Getty Images; p. 23 © 2011 GoDaddy.com, Inc. All rights reserved.; p. 26 Courtesy of ReverbNation.com; p. 29 Epoxydude/Getty Images; p. 32 Justin Sullivan/Getty Images; p. 35 Tim Ireland/PA Photos/Landov; p. 38 Burazin/Stone/Getty Images; p. 42 courtesy of MySongStore.com; p. 45 © El Tiempo/GDA/ZumaPress.com; p. 49 Jupiterimages/BananaStock/Thinkstock; back cover and interior graphic elements © www.istockphoto.com/Adam Gryko (radio dial), © www.istockphoto.com/Tomasz Zajaczkowski (amp), © www.istockphoto.com/sammyc (drum set silhouette), Shutterstock.com (cable, frequency bar), © www.istockphoto.com/spxChrome (stage pass), © www.istockphoto.com/Bryan Faust (foot pedal).

Designer: Nicole Russo; Editor: Nicholas Croce;
Photo Researcher: Karen Huang